# THE BACKGROUND
# OF THE
# FRENCH REVOLUTION

*By*

## STANLEY J. IDZERDA

Michigan State University

*A Publication of the American Historical Association's*

SERVICE CENTER FOR TEACHERS OF HISTORY

400 A Street, S. E., Washington 3, D. C.

THE MACMILLAN COMPANY, NEW YORK
COLLIER-MACMILLAN LIMITED, LONDON

Library of Congress catalog card number: 59-10401

The Macmillan Company, New York
Collier-Macmillan Canada, Ltd., Toronto, Ontario
DIVISIONS OF THE CROWELL-COLLIER PUBLISHING COMPANY

*Printed in the United States of America*

## COMMITTEE ON TEACHING OF THE
## AMERICAN HISTORICAL ASSOCIATION

# THE BACKGROUND
# OF THE
# FRENCH REVOLUTION

*by*

## STANLEY J. IDZERDA

Michigan State University

*Publication Number 21*

SERVICE CENTER FOR TEACHERS OF HISTORY
*A Service of the American Historical Association*

## THE MACMILLAN COMPANY

*60 Fifth Avenue, New York*

The American Historical Association, because of its continuing interest in the teaching of history in the schools of the United States, has established the Service Center for Teachers of History in an effort to offer constructive assistance in solving some of the problems which today beset the classroom teacher. One of the programs being sponsored by the Service Center is the preparation of a series of pamphlets, each containing a concise summary of publications reflecting recent research and new interpretations in a particular field of history.

Since many secondary school teachers have neither the time nor opportunity to read widely in monographic literature, these pamphlets have been specifically designed to meet classroom teachers' needs. Each pamphlet purports to bring the reader abreast of current interpretations and significant writings in a specific field of historical study. Our aim is, in short, to help the teachers help themselves by keeping up to date in their fields of interest. It is our sincere hope that this will materially benefit the teacher and thereby contribute to the enrichment of classroom instruction. The extent to which the project is successful will be measured by the degree to which the regrettable gap between the teacher of history in the school and the specialist in historical research is narrowed.

WALTER RUNDELL, JR.

# THE BACKGROUND OF THE FRENCH REVOLUTION

*By Stanley J. Idzerda*

On September 4, 1958, Charles de Gaulle delivered a speech urging his listeners to vote "yes" on the draft constitution for the Fifth Republic. He began by saying:

> It was at a time when it had to reform or be shattered that our people first had recourse to the Republic. Until then, down the centuries, the Old Regime had achieved the unity and maintained the integrity of France. But, while a great tidal wave was forming in the depths, it showed itself incapable of adapting to a new world. It was then—in the midst of national turmoil and of foreign war—that the Republic appeared. It was the sovereignty of the people, the call of liberty, the hope of justice. That is what it was to remain through all the restless vicissitudes of its history. Today, as much as ever, that is what we want it to remain.

If an Englishman were to make similar references to the revolution of 1688 or an American politician summarized the background of the revolution of 1776 during a political speech, most of their listeners would accept the statements as part of the harmless rhetoric one expects on such occasions. But De Gaulle's capsule history of eighteenth-century France was more than rhetoric to his listeners. For the Frenchman, *histoire contemporaine* dates from the French Revolution. Many of the living issues of the eighteenth century and the solutions offered by the Revolution remain alive in France still. Thus, for the French voter, knowing where political candidates stand on the issue of the Revolution and its background is important.

The analysis of the French Revolution and its causes is not an activity of recent origin. From the outset, the Revolution was recognized as one of the great pivotal events of modern history, and analysis, both within and without France, began while the Revolution was still in its infancy. The analysis continues to this day. The historiography of the background of the Revolution, of the Revolution itself, and of its impact upon France during every generation up to the present, has the aspects of a minor industry.[1]

---

[1] C. Brinton, *The Anatomy of Revolution* (rev. ed.; New York, 1952); P. Farmer,

If the average American of De Gaulle's age were asked to summarize the background of the French Revolution as it was taught to him in school, his reply might run something like this:

> Eighteenth-century France was composed of three rigid classes. The most numerous, the backbone of the nation, was the Third Estate, led by the "rising middle class." The Second Estate was composed of nobles, most of whom lived at Versailles, while they squandered the resources provided by the Third Estate. The First Estate, constituting the clergy, had lost most of its medieval functions, with the exception of taxes which came from the Third Estate. The Revolution was owing to the inability of an essentially corrupt monarchy to withstand the demands or meet the needs of the Third Estate as expressed by such agents of the Enlightenment as Voltaire and Rousseau.

During the last 50 years, historians on both sides of the Atlantic have made such a simplified analysis impossible. Particularly noticeable is the tendency to study eighteenth-century France for its own sake, without making the assumption that Frenchmen before 1789 were looking forward to, or planning for, the Great Revolution. Also, in more recent years, the emphasis has been upon careful social and economic studies; most of these recent works insist upon the complexity of institutions and motives rather than their simplicity.

*French Society and Government*

In spite of disastrous wars and indifferent leadership, France remained the greatest and most modern of any of the states on the continent during the eighteenth century. French cultural dominance seemed assured, and France's size and wealth, coupled with a stable social structure, seemed to presage continued growth and recovery from even the most costly wars.

Although the eighteenth century was a pre-statistical era, the best educated guesses place its population toward the end of the century

*France Reviews Its Revolutionary Origins* (New York, 1944); S. Mellon, *The Political Uses of History: A Study of Historians in the French Restoration* (Stanford, 1958); A. Cobban, *Historians and the Causes of the French Revolution* (rev. ed.; London, 1958); L. Gottschalk, "Phillipe Sagnac and the Causes of the French Revolution," *Journal of Modern History*, XX (1948), 137–148; J. L. B. Atkinson, "Taine on the French Revolution: A Study in Historiographic Controversy," *Historian*, XV (1953), 188–216; R. Herr, "Histoire littéraire: Daniel Mornet and the French Enlightenment," *Journal of Modern History*, XXIV (1952), 152–166.

at about 25,000,000. Easily 97 per cent of this population were members of the Third Estate. The chief unity that can be ascribed to this group is that they were not members of the nobility, nor were they clergy or members of a religious order.

The tendency to identify the Third Estate and the "middle class," along with the assumption that most of the history of France was made in Paris or Versailles, have both tended to disappear during recent years. Increasing interest in the rocklike substratum of French society, the peasantry, has been evidenced in the careful studies of their numbers, distribution, and status.

But even the peasantry cannot be grouped together as a unit. Although conditions varied widely in each section of France, perhaps one-twentieth owned their land outright, another one-quarter were tenant farmers, one-half farmed land on a sharecropping basis, about one-fifth were landless agricultural laborers. Serfdom had well-nigh disappeared; the highest estimate of the number of serfs is about one-twentieth of the rural population.

But feudalism remained to confuse the very meaning of the term "ownership" of land. If one included the number of peasants who held their land as apparent owners and were able to pass it on to their children, but who at the same time had to pay various feudal rents and dues, one might raise the number of "owners" to something close to one-third of the peasantry. Also, while the nobility held about 20 per cent of the tillable soil, and the church perhaps 7 per cent, not all the peasants who were tenants or sharecroppers farmed land belonging to the church or the nobility. In some areas the peasant might own a small parcel, be a tenant on another parcel and have tenants or sharecroppers on yet others. When a wealthy member of the bourgeoisie bought a fief, he often played the role of the noble with regard to the manorial rights on the land farmed by the peasants.

Owing to the lack of detailed studies for every area of France, both the status and condition of the French peasant are still the subject of discussion. That he was seldom bound to the soil as a serf is usually agreed upon, but whether or not he was prosperous is an open question, confused by the fact that, to avoid the multitude of taxes and assessments, the standard gambit of the peasant was to "dress poor" and "talk poor." The contrary evidence indicates that

more and more peasants were making the countless small sacrifices
necessary to add to their land holdings all during the eighteenth
century.

When the condition of the French peasant is compared to that
of peasants on the rest of the continent, there is little doubt that
the French peasant was much the better off. Perhaps the best evidence is that the number and severity of famines in the French
countryside were reduced during the century, that there was a
steady increase in the rate of population growth, and that, during
the last two reigns before the Revolution, there was no serious up-
rising of the peasantry.

The eighteenth-century peasants' wants or desires can be easily
summarized: to own more land, and to own it free of manorial
restrictions and obligations as well as with a reduced load of taxes
imposed by the state. Perhaps a close second was the wish to pre-
vent any instability in the market for the products of his labors.

There is little or no evidence that the mass of the rural population
saw any common cause with the rest of the Third Estate, even
though they often had similar interests; considerable numbers of
the peasantry had such small holdings that they found it necessary
to pursue a trade in the nearest town or village, and members of
the bourgeoisie were owners of perhaps 20 per cent of the land.

Yet the nearly two million members of the Third Estate who
lived in towns and cities, the burgeoisie, were far removed in way of
life and aspirations from those who tilled the soil for a livelihood.
At the same time, the range of position, wealth, and power among
bourgeoisie was such that it is impossible to call them "the rising
middle class" with the pretense of unity of aim. If anything, divisions among the bourgeoisie were more numerous than those among
the peasantry. At the top of the economic heap were the great finan-
ciers who lived very much like nobles, below them came wholesale
merchants, shopkeepers, artisans, and laborers. A similar, and almost parallel hierarchy could be found among the professionals:
writers, lawyers, doctors, and minor public functionaries.

Elinor Barber has shown rather convincingly (*The Bourgeoisie
in Eighteenth-century France*) that the bourgeoisie accepted the
society of Estates, and the divisions within the Third Estate. Somewhat paradoxically, the chief desire of the bourgeoisie was for

social mobility founded upon wealth, ability, or function. The middle and upper bourgeoisie recognized and respected careful distinctions in status among themselves, but at the same time aspired to move up one notch in the social ladder through marriage, the purchase of a noble estate, or the purchase of an office which gave noble prerogatives and privileges, no matter how petty. In much the same way that the peasantry resented increasing stringency in the application of manorial dues and rents during the eighteenth century, the many educated or wealthy bourgeoisie resented the tendency for the crown and the nobility to close off opportunities for upward mobility during the same period.

Possibly the desire for any office or any increased social status, no matter how small, moved beyond the simple demand for nobility, since almost any municipal or state functionary, as well as even the lowest order of nobles, were released from some of the taxes and obligations incumbent upon the rest of the Third Estate.

Although great numbers of the bourgeoisie hoped to become members of the nobility, at the same time probably the friction between these two groups was the most sensed during the eighteenth century. The status and power of the nobility had been diminished considerably during the seventeenth century, while it is doubtful that their aspirations had done anything but increase. Again, to speak of them as a single "class" or Estate, in any excepting the strictly legal sense, is difficult. Of some 80,000 members of the nobility, the range in economic status ran from royal luxury to rural poverty. Only 4,000 were eligible to live at Versailles or pay court there; the rest lacked sufficient "degrees" of nobility. Within the ranks, the old noble families, the great magistrate families, and the petty nobility who had some provincial or municipal function, many careful and invidious distinctions were made.

The legal unity of the Second Estate was not unimportant; every member of the nobility had considerable privileges and exemptions from duties and obligations which encumbered the Third Estate. The presumption was that in return for these privileges, the nobility would defend the state and help rule it. In fact, the noble function in warfare differed from the Third Estate only in that positions of command were usually restricted to the nobility, especially in the army. As for government, the more recent studies agree with the older that the functions of the nobles in government had been drastically reduced during the seventeenth century.

Much has been written concerning the "feudal reaction" of the nobility in the eighteenth century. While the peasantry wanted land, and the bourgeoisie wanted status mobility, it seems clear that the nobility wanted to maintain their privileges and even renew many which were presumed to have existed during the middle ages. The nobility attempted to revive, strengthen, or tighten their manorial rights and privileges and to raise the dues or rents on the land they held. As for positions of control within the state, not a single bishop of the church in 1789 came from the commoners, and during the whole century there were increasing attempts by the nobility, through the courts which they controlled, to participate in some of the actions of the crown.

Nominally, the old nobility were disdainful of the relatively new group of nobles who were the magistrates. Franklin Ford has shown, however, that by 1750 the nobility of the robe in the great courts had made common cause with the nobility of the sword in the direction of sustaining or increasing the noble prerogative and privilege in the government, as well as other spheres of life.[2]

It was once commonly assumed that the First Estate, including all the clergy and members of religious orders, was a reasonably unified and privileged group which would make common cause with the nobility. Again, the scholarship of recent decades has reinforced the view that diversity and cross-currents existed in the First Estate as well; if it was a monolithic organization, this was true only in outer appearance.

[2] F. L. Ford, *Robe and Sword: The Regrouping of the French Aristocracy After Louis XIV* (Cambridge, Mass., 1953); E. Barber, *The Bourgeoisie in Eighteenth-Century France* (Princeton, 1955); A. Goodwin (ed.), *The European Nobility in the Eighteenth Century* (London, 1953); J. Ellul, *Histoire des Institutions*, Vol. II (Paris, 1956); P. Sagnac, *La formation de la société française moderne*, Vol. II, (Paris, 1946); H. Sée, *Histoire économique de la France*, Vol. I (Paris, 1948); M. Bloch, *Les caractères originaux de l'histoire rural française* (rev. ed.; Paris, 1952); A. Soboul, "The French Rural Community in the Eighteenth and Nineteenth Centuries," *Past and Present*, no. 10 (1956), 78–95; M. Bluche, "L'origine sociale du personnel ministeriel français au XVIIIe siècle," *Bulletin de la Société d'Histoire Moderne*, second series, №1 (Jan., 1957), 9–13; J. Bourgeois-Pichat, "Evolution de la population en France depuis le 18e siècle," *Population*, VI (1951), 635–60; R. Baehrel, "La mortalité sous l'ancien régime. Remarques inquiètes," *Annales: Économies, Sociétés, Civilisations*, XII (1957), 85–98.

As an institution, the church was probably the single wealthiest proprietor in France by 1789. The amount and quality of the land held by the church has been revised downward drastically until it is now agreed that it held about 7 per cent. However, the tithes it collected, the inheritances it received, and the property it held in towns and cities more than made up in value for the landed wealth it did not possess.

Of the total of 130,000 monks, nuns, and priests, about 60,000 were "secular" including the parish priests, bishops; about 70,000 were monks and nuns in orders. The functions and conditions of existence of the whole 130,000 differed as widely as their attitudes toward their tasks. Part of the wealth of the church supported some 2,000 hospitals which were maintained by some 35,000 of the "regular" clergy, while there were perhaps 75,000 students in the 600 colleges maintained by the church. However, another part of the vast wealth of the church went to support some wealthy bishops and abbots in conditions of luxury which were a major scandal, considering the poverty of the parish clergy. Also, many of the monasteries in the countryside seemed to exercise their manorial privileges over the land they held even more stringently than many of the nobles.

Outside of agreement that the function of the First Estate was the care of souls, charity, education, and hospital work, there was little if any unity of social origin of its members or even unity regarding dogma and the organization of the church. If someone in the year 1750 had said he expected a revolution any moment, the revolution he had in mind would relate to the violent disputes over Jansenism which had been condemned by the Papacy but still had many supporters and opponents in France. As for the government of the church, the Gallicans expected the crown to verify all major appointments and to determine the attitude of the French church toward the Papacy. Many of the parish priests were attracted by "Richerism," which in effect would give the parish clergy more control and voice in the government of the church in France. One result of these divisions was the increased bitterness of the parish clergy; another was the expulsion of the Jesuits in 1764.

It is, of course, practically impossible to examine the conscience of any person or group of people, and it is difficult to know exactly the condition of religion in France in the eighteenth century. As for the attitude of the people toward the church, the peasant might accept and admire the parish priest, while detesting a nearby monastery which was imposing manorial dues upon the land held by the peasants. The peasants were not aware of the high style of life led by some bishops, but these bishops, and other high church officials who held multiple offices which brought income but no duties, caused resentment among the parish clergy and the urban middle classes. On the other hand, members of religious orders who worked in the cities performed functions felt chiefly by the poor. The more recent judgments of both Catholic and anticlerical historians tend to agree that the majority of Frenchmen were reasonably pious, and piety more often drifted into indifference rather than opposition to the church.

If the Catholic clergy in France were agreed upon anything, it was that Catholicism should be given a privileged and protected position within the state, and that the 40,000 Jews and 200,000 Protestants remain, in effect, second class citizens. There was less persecution of these two latter groups during the later eighteenth century than had been the case earlier, but this has been less often attributed to tolerance than to indifference.[3]

At the top of the whole social and political structure was the crown. Much has been written about enlightened despotism in the eighteenth century, and we occasionally make the easy inference that France was a state noted for this kind of rule. It may be that Louis XIV was the pattern for the "enlightened despots" of the eighteenth century, but his two successors were only inadvertently enlightened and only rarely despotic. The church and the nobility protested regularly that the king was the sole ruler in the state, that his power was absolute and came from God, but the number of disputes or difficulties the crown had with the first two Estates seemed to belie their protestations.

[3] R. R. Palmer, *Catholics and Unbelievers in Eighteenth-Century France* (Princeton, 1939); C. E. Elwell, *The Influence of the Enlightenment on the Catholic Theory of Religious Education in France* (Cambridge, Mass., 1944); B. C. Poland, *French Protestantism and the French Revolution* (Princeton, 1957); A. Latreille, *L'Église Catholique et la Révolution française*, Vol. I (Paris, 1946); E. Préclin and E. Jarry, *Les Luttes politiques et doctrinales aux XVIIe et XVIIIe siècles* (Paris, 1955).

Obviously, in a hereditary monarchy much depends upon the personal qualities of those who succeed to the throne. The historical judgments passed upon the personalities of Louis XV and Louis XVI have changed but little in a century; if one bothered to count all the articles and books written about the French court one would probably find historians have been more interested in Louis XV's mistresses and in Louis XVI's wife than in the kings. This interest points up the chief defect of the crown; intrigue is perhaps an unavoidable curse of any court, but during the eighteenth century intrigue seems to have been erected into a central principle of government. To get an inside account of the major and minor decisions of state one must know a very great deal about the mistresses of one king and the wife of another.

Two changes in historical judgment are evident. First, the notion that the French became politically unstable only after the upheaval of the French Revolution is giving way to the view that the French have always been difficult to rule. Second, it is more often realized that the fiscal and political legacy left by Louis XIV would have taxed the powers of a genius, and that hereditary, divine right monarchy has produced no larger proportion of geniuses than any other form of government. Finally, for all the real defects of Louis XIV's successors, administrative and institutional studies have shown that real effort was made to modernize the French state, and that some progress was made.

The "progress" would have to be in the direction of reducing political particularism and localism, reform of a fantastically complicated and inequitable tax structure, and the encouragement of industry and trade, all overseen by an effective administrative group under the crown. Historians have become somewhat less critical of relatively small achievements on the part of the crown because it is being realized that France was not a unitary state on the twentieth-century pattern.

These same historians are more critical of the two privileged groups, and especially of the nobility. Almost any change would mean that the fiscal, social, or political privileges of the nobility and the church would be lessened, and the nobility in the Parisian and provincial courts (the *parlements*) were the spearhead of organized opposition. The *parlements* could and did join with the church in condemning writings which tended to be subversive of the status quo, but quite often their own legal decisions became public manifestos against the "despotism" of the crown. If there was a "revolutionary class" in France during the forty years before the Revolution, present day historians would say that this class was none other than those nobles who controlled the courts, and pleaded for liberty against royal despotism. That the "liberty" they sought was the strengthening of their own privileges and prerogatives at all costs is quite clear. France had many aspects of a feudal society during the eighteenth century, overlapping a great deal that was modern. The attempts of the nobles to restore those elements of feudalism favorable to themselves certainly weakened any reforming efforts of the crown, and seem to have been one of the major factors in the final collapse of the monarchy at the end of the century.[4]

## The Age of Reason

Among the long-range or long-term antecedents of the Revolution, the "Enlightenment" or "Age of Reason" still takes first place in importance, even though recent work on political strife between the crown and the nobility has tended to diminish its pre-eminence. The more partisan accounts of the nineteenth century were wont to give the men of the Enlightenment either too much praise or too much blame. One school was inclined to think that all that was

[4] G. P. Gooch, *Louis XV, the Monarchy in Decline* (New York, 1956); G. P. Gooch, "Maria Theresa and Marie Antoinette," in *Maria Theresa and Other Studies* (New York, 1951); A. Castelot, *Queen of France* (New York, 1957); B. Fay, *Louis XVI, ou la fin d'un monde*, (Paris, 1955); E. Dard, *La Chute de la royauté* (Paris, 1950); G. Lefebvre, "Le Despotisme éclairé," *Annales historiques de la Révolution française*, XXI (1949), 97–115; H. B. Hill, "French Constitutionalism: Old Regime and Revolutionary," *Journal of Modern History*, XXI (1949), 222–227; L. Gottschalk, "The French Parlements and Judicial Review," *Journal of the History of Ideas*, V (1944), 105–112; A. Cobban, "The Parlements of France in the Eighteenth Century," *History*, XXXV (1950), 64–80; J. Egret, "L'aristocratie parlementaire française à la fin de l'ancien régime," *Revue historique*, CCVII (1952), 1–14.

For the problems of royal administration and administrative reform, see D. Dakin, *Turgot and the Ancien Regime in France* (London, 1939); S. T. McCloy, *Government Assistance in Eighteenth-century France* (Durham, 1946); P. W. Bamford, *Forests and French Sea Power* (Toronto, 1956); G. T. Matthews, *The Royal General Farms in Eighteenth-century France* (New York, 1958); G. Weulersse, *La physiocratie sous les ministères de Turgot et de Necker* (Paris, 1950); H. Freville, *L'Intendance de Bretagne (1689–1790)* (3 vols.; Rennes, 1953).

good in the eighteenth century and in the Revolution was owing to the planning and the writing of those *philosophes* who were active during the middle third of the century. The opposing school credited the *philosophes* with the destruction of Old France and all that was good in it. On occasions the intellectual leaders have had ascribed to them both a level of organization, and a desire to "plot" the disintegration of the church and the monarchy, that even Catholic historians and royalists today would not accept.

The Enlightenment was an age during which a larger and larger proportion of the population of France living in towns wrote or read about criticisms and plans for the reform of society on the basis of reason, utility, decency, tolerance, and freedom. Outside of the salons in the few major cities, and the discussions in the provincial academies, the movement was chiefly literary. During the first third of the century, apparently more of the critics were noble than bourgeois and their work, especially when it was critical of the established religion, was distributed in a clandestine fashion. The scope and freedom for criticism of almost any institution was vastly increased after 1750, owing in part to indifference among those who had the powers of censorship, as well as to the acceptance of many of these ideas by the literate population.

The French historian Hazard has tried to show that all the factors present in the Enlightenment developed during the last decades of the reign of Louis XIV, while Carl Becker seemed inclined to think that the *philosophes* had more in common with the world view of the Middle Ages than with the nineteenth or twentieth centuries. Recent scholarship is inclined to give more credit for originality and seriousness of purpose to the men of the Enlightenment than had been the case earlier. Diderot, in particular, has gained in prestige as a thinker over the past twenty years. The reevaluation of Voltaire does not diminish his importance, but it seems agreed that his forte was brilliant and coruscating polemic rather than original philosophy. At the same time, it would be a mistake to assume unity of purpose or thought among the *philosophes*: Rousseau, who emphasized sentiment much more often than he did reason, broke with the other major leaders of the reformist school and had many minor followers. In any event, individual *philosophes* could express thoughts apparently inconsistent with their own ideas of progress and the pursuit of reason, and at the same time disagree violently with other *philosophes*.

The consistency of these critics lay in the fact that all desired social and personal reform, based upon human and worldly goals. While many were deists and some were atheists, they attacked not so much religion as the practices of religious institutions. They wanted a society in which privilege without accompanying significant functions was abolished, a doctrine which would have considerable appeal for those talented members of the middle and lower-middle classes who were blocked in advancement because of their unfortunate choice of parents. In spite of the accusations or the claims made in the nineteenth century, the *philosophes* were not concerned with, or interested in, political revolutions as such. They seem to accept the monarchy and the ordering of society, only asking that it be "enlightened." Perhaps Turgot was the only one of the great economic thinkers of the eighteenth century who actually held any significant office, but the rationalization of government functions and the growth of humanitarian ideals and activities seems to be owing, in a large measure, to the publicity that the *philosophes* gave to these ideals.

As for the effect upon the general public, studies of reading habits of the middle bourgeoisie indicate that they probably looked into Diderot and D'Alembert's *Encyclopedia* more for information than for subversive philosophy. At the same time, it seems clear that the large bulk of reading matter among those who bought books consisted of works of popular piety, sentimental romances, histories, and works containing practical information. If there was a surge of reason or rationality, it seemed equally countered by pietism and sentiment.[5]

[5] L. Crocker, *The Embattled Philosopher, A Life of Denis Diderot* (East Lansing, 1954); A. M. Wilson, *Diderot, The Testing Years, 1713–1759* (New York, 1957); F. C. Green, *Jean-Jacques Rousseau* (Cambridge, 1955); A. Vartanian, *Diderot and Descartes* (Princeton, 1953); G. R. Havens, *The Age of Ideas* (New York, 1955); K. Martin, *The Rise of French Liberal Thought* (rev. ed.; New York, 1956); S. T. McCloy, *The Humanitarian Movement in Eighteenth-century France* (Lexington, Ky., 1957); C. Becker, *The Heavenly City of the Eighteenth-century Philosophers* (New Haven, 1932); R. O. Rockwood (ed.), *Carl Becker's Heavenly City Revisited* (Ithaca, 1958); C. Frankel, *The Faith of Reason: The Idea of Progress in the French Enlightenment* (New York, 1948); R. V. Sampson, *Progress in the Age of Reason, The Seventeenth*

## The Influence of America

Possibly the most significant influence of the *philosophes* derived from their interest in countries and cultures other than their own. The eighteenth century has often been accused of being an "unhistorical" era, but the outpouring of histories, and historical commentaries, as well as the popularity of such work during the "Age of Reason" is rivalled only by the nineteenth century. Perhaps the writers of the eighteenth century were "unhistorical" in our sense of the term because they seldom made much pretense of writing "objective" history. The past was to serve as an example to the present, and contemporary history or social analysis seemed more often written to defend the status quo, reaction, or reform.

In much the same way as the *philosophes* and their opponents used the scientific revolution of the seventeenth century to argue the pros and cons of religious, social, and political questions, the Far East, the South Sea islands, the Roman Republic, the Middle Ages and England and America became foils for those disputing conditions in France. Whether any of these cultures offered anything positive was an open question; classical authors were used to prove whatever the writer wanted to prove at the moment, and while there was a good deal of "Anglomania" in eighteenth-century France, it was partly balanced by "Anglophobia."

America shared with England a dominant place in the interests of those who were seeking examples for the superiority of French

*Century to the Present Day* (Cambridge, Mass., 1956); P. Hazard, *The European Mind, 1680–1715* (New Haven, 1953); P. Hazard, *European Thought in the Eighteenth Century: From Montesquieu to Lessing* (New Haven, 1954); D. Mornet, *Les origines intellectuelles de la Révolution française* (rev. ed.; Paris, 1954); H. Vyverberg, *Historical Pessimism in the French Enlightenment* (Cambridge, Mass., 1958); D. T. Pottinger, *The French Book Trade in the Ancien Regime* (Cambridge, Mass., 1958); I. Cumming, *Helvetius* (London, 1955); H. Peyre, "Influence of Eighteenth-century Ideas on the French Revolution," *Journal of the History of Ideas*, X (1949), 63–87; R. N. Stromberg, "History in the Eighteenth Century," *Journal of the History of Ideas*, XII (1951), 295–304; L. G. Crocker, "The Problem of Truth and Falsehood in the Age of the Enlightenment," *Journal of the History of Ideas*, XIV (1953), 575–603; P. Gay, "The Enlightenment in the History of Political Theory," *Political Science Quarterly*, LXIX (1954), 374–89; A. M. Wilson, "The Age of the Enlightenment and the Contemporary World," *William and Mary Quarterly*, XIV (1957), 88–97; G. Lefebvre, "La Révolution française et le Rationalisme," *Annales historiques de la Révolution française*, XVIII (1946), 4–34.

civilization or the need for its reform. That all interest was not favorable to the New World is demonstrated by Jefferson's defense of it against Europeans who would derogate its fine qualities. Yet, for all the influence of America as an example to be avoided or followed, there seems little doubt that the most important influence of America as a precursor of the Revolution was the French involvement in the American Revolution.

It is agreed that the extensive support of the French monarchy in the American cause was not so much an approval of republicanism or democracy as it was an attempt on the part of France to redress the balance of power with England. An England weakened by the loss of colonies would be hurt both politically and economically. At the same time, the Franco-American alliance of 1778 made Louis XVI a partner in revolution. When Benjamin Franklin, the very epitome of "Enlightenment," served as an envoy in France he was lionized by all elements of society. Members of the French aristocracy who were later leaders of liberal elements during the early period of the French Revolution served as officers in the American Army. However, the officers who came to America sought glory and the defeat of a traditional enemy, rather than the fulfillment of any philosophical principles. This is not to say that they were not affected by their experience in the New World. Perhaps more important than the relatively small officer corps were the rest of the eighteen thousand veterans of the land war in America. They returned to their homes having seen the common man in America a freeholder on his soil and enjoying both prosperity and liberty. It has been suggested that wherever there were geographical concentrations of these French veterans of the American Revolution in France during the early years of the French Revolution, that area was more radical than others.[6]

[6] J. H. Brummfitt, *Voltaire, Historian* (New York, 1958); M. L. Dufrenoy, *L'Orient romanesque en France, 1704–1789* (Vol. I; Montreal, 1946); L. Villard, *La France et les États-Unis: échanges et rencontres, 1524–1800* (Paris, 1952); D. Echeverria, *Mirage in the West: A History of the French Image of American Society to 1815* (Princeton, 1957); A. O. Aldridge, *Franklin and His French Contemporaries* (New York, 1957); L. Gottschalk, *Lafayette Joins the American Army* (Chicago, 1937); L. Gottschalk, *Lafayette Between the American and the French Revolution* (Chicago, 1950); L. Gottschalk, "The Place of the American Revolution in the Causal Pattern of the French Revolution," *American Friends of Lafayette* (1948); D. M. Clark, "British

*The Economic Crisis*

Whatever the presumed change in attitudes on the part of the participants in the American Revolution and the impact of the American Constitution of 1787 may have been, the most significant aspect of the participation in the American war was the fact that this participation doubled the national debt of France. The huge debt incurred was probably the major factor in the last fiscal and economic crisis faced by the crown in the eighteenth century.

R. W. Greenlaw has recently edited eleven excerpts from the work of French historians relating to the economic origins of the French Revolution. These neatly demonstrate the pendulum swings in historical opinion over the past century. The issue has always been confused by the relative economic well-being of France, leading some to aver that a revolution becomes possible only when there is a momentary lull in a rising tide of prosperity.

The fiscal problems of the government at the end of the century have seldom been in dispute, but the state of the economy was more often based upon contemporary opinion than upon empirical evidence. This lack of evidence has been in a large measure rectified by the two most significant and controversial studies of recent years relating to the economic background of the Revolution, both by C. E. Labrousse. Labrousse has concentrated upon statistical studies of prices and business cycles in the period before the Revolution, and he concludes that the French economy, with the exception of foreign trade, was in a slow but steady decline after 1774, and that this decline was occasionally exaggerated in its effect by poor harvests. In particular, the bad harvests of 1788–89, coinciding with rising prices, were responsible for unrest and misery among the peasants and the urban laborers. Labrousse does grant a general improvement in conditions in the eighteenth century, but he holds that the short-run economic decline and the harvest crises just be-

Opinion of Franco-American Relations, 1775-95," *William and Mary Quarterly,* IV (1947), 305–316; F. McDonald, "The Relation of the French Peasant Veterans of the American Revolution to the Fall of Feudalism in France, 1789–92," *Agricultural History,* XXV (1951), 151–161; J. Godechot, "Les combattants de la guerre de I'Indépendance des États-Unis et les troubles agraires en France de 1789 à 1792," *Annales historiques de la Révolution française,* XXVIII (1956), 292–294; F. Acomb, *Anglophobia in France, 1763–1789* (Durham, 1950).

fore the Revolution built up an explosive situation that could play havoc with political decisions. Although his theory and methods have been severely criticized by D. S. Landes, it appears that most French historians accept both Labrousse's methods and his conclusions. The question still remains: what was the specific weight of the economic crisis of 1788–89 upon the outbreak of the Revolution?[7]

## The Opening Phases of the French Revolution

Historians are in the main agreed that the tensions, the criticisms, the dissatisfaction, and the thwarted desires of many elements of French society were not in themselves sufficient to cause a revolution. Even Labrousse does not claim that the major economic crisis, arising from the support given America or the bad harvests of 1787–89, was a necessary "cause" of the Revolution which began in 1789.

A bald summary of current historical opinion concerning the immediate antecedents of the Revolution might run as follows: the economic and fiscal crisis caused either fear or hardship at every level of society; the attempts of the crown to solve the problem, or at least alleviate the crisis, were blocked by the aristocracy; the last phase of the "nobles revolt" was the insistence of the *parlements* that the Three Estates be convened in an Estates General, which they thought would be controlled by the first two Estates; the Third Estate seized the leadership of the Estates General, and, with some supporters from the nobility and many from the clergy, organized a Consituent Assembly. The Revolution was in full tide.

Of course, many changes and variations are rung upon each of

---

[7] R. W. Greenlaw, (ed.), *The Economic Origins of the French Revolution: Poverty or Prosperity?* (Boston, 1958); C. E. Labrousse, *La crise de l'économie française à la fin de l'ancien régime et au début de la révolution* (Paris, 1944); C. E. Labrousse, *Esquisse de mouvement des prix et des revenus en France au XVIIIe siècle* (2 vols.; Paris, 1933); D. S. Landes, "The Statistical Study of French Crises," *Journal of Economic History,* X (1950), 195–211; A. G. Pundt, "French Agriculture and the Industrial Crisis of 1788," *Journal of Political Economy,* XLIX (1941), 849–874; T. F. Power, Jr., "Emergency Relief in France in 1788," *Journal of Modern History,* XIII (1941), 218–224; F. Acomb, "Unemployment and Relief in Champagne, 1788," *Journal of Modern History,* XI (1939), 41–48; G. E. Rudé, "Prices, Wages and Popular Movements in Paris during the French Revolution," *Economic History Review,* VI (1954), 246–267.

these fundamental elements. None of the developments in the two years before 1789 were "necessary," because there is no evidence that anyone desired or planned a revolution; if such evidence were found, it seems dubious that the plan would have fitted the events as they unrolled. What is perhaps most interesting is that the nobles appeared to be leading a united nation even up to the point when they insisted upon the convocation of the Estates General.

At that time it became strikingly clear that the *parlements* had no intention of giving the Third Estate any significant role beyond that of ratifying the decisions of the first two Estates. Much of the criticism stemming from the Third Estate during the latter half of the century indicated that they were not satisfied with their subordinate role. Had either the crown or the aristocracy made a genuine effort to join forces with the Third Estate, there might still have been a "revolution" but it would have had an entirely different character.

Few responsible historians today would declare that the rush of events between 1789 and the advent of Napoleon followed any remorseless logic necessary to the French Revolution. It the Revolution is divided into a series of stages, these are often matters of convenience, and at each turning point there is the question of changing intellectual climate and material conditions, as well as the real alternatives that may have been chosen by the major and minor actors on the scene. If this view is pushed a little further, it becomes difficult to speak of "the" French Revolution in the narrow sense as a historical event with a single meaning.

For the opening phase in 1788–89 perhaps three questions are most often raised. Granting the aristocracy triggered the Revolution, which class or classes are most significant immediately thereafter? Liberal orthodoxy of the nineteenth century made the "middle class" the leader, while recognizing occasional unfortunate irruptions of "the mob." The later Marxist orthodoxy saw original bourgeois leadership which regularly thwarted the later development of a "peoples" revolution. Contemporary scholarship suggests that riots and spontaneous or loosely organized violence on the part of the peasantry or the laborers and journeymen in the cities played an important role from 1788 on. That even the aristocracy incited riots to forward their ends seems clearly established. From the very beginning to the end of the Revolution the stirrings at the bottom of society had a palpable influence upon the actions of those who were in the seats of power and those who sought power. It would be misleading to say that the mass of the population played a significant role only after the aristocracy and the bourgeoisie had occupied the stage.

As for the leadership of the "middle class," the term is so ambiguous in this context as to define nothing. Certainly the upper bourgeoisie did not dominate or lead any phase of the Revolution, and the artisan or shopkeeper had even less to do with the shaping of events. In his discussion of the "myth" of the Revolution, Cobban has shown that the petty official, and the small town lawyer dominated the Consituent Assembly; many of the clergy who went over to the Third Estate had similar backgrounds. Even so, the lists of grievances (*cahiers des doléances*) drawn up during the elections for the Estates General give no evidence of "class consciousness." Those written for the members of the Third Estate usually list specific grievances; if a general tenor is derived from them, it is that privileges without concomitant duties and obligations should be abolished. Beyond this, there is the tendency to see the interests of France as a "nation" rather than as a hierarchical society bound together by personal ties.

This leads to the second, and perhaps more bitterly contested question: what was the influence of the ideas current during the Enlightenment on the course of the Revolution? To be sure, the action of the peasantry influenced the revolutionaries to remove the very kind of feudal dues and restrictions opposed by the *philosophes*, but no one has claimed that the largely illiterate peasants spent their evenings reading Voltaire. On the other hand, we do not need to be told when we have a toothache: the peasant could feel the tax load and observe obvious inequities that affected him. As for the dominant group in the Constituent Assembly their desires for "careers open to talent" were clear enough, and they probably got much of their vocabulary and justification from the very climate of opinion created by the *philosophes*. By the time the Revolution reached the stage when Rousseau and Voltaire were lionized, a cause and effect relationship was being claimed between their work and the work of the revolutionaries. However, at that stage, these were merely names serving as political rallying centers and justifications of political faith.

The third question relates to the exigencies or accidents of political leadership during the decade 1780–1790. For all their very real individualism, the French showed remarkable capacities for common devotion to an idea or political leader after the Revolution began. Although seldom blessed with a king worth following, historians agree that even during the eighteenth century the population remained loyal to the institution of monarchy. Historical suppositions are usually fruitless guessing games and few historians indulge in them. However, when one considers the leadership potential still latent in the crown, and the fact that during the years 1787–89, indecision, inaction, and vacillation remained characteristic of Louis XVI, one is not inclined to regard the events leading to the collapse of the monarchy as inevitable.

Although C. E. Labrousse's analysis of the economic crisis in the years at the end of the Old Regime just before the Revolution has been the most influential single work relating to the background of the Revolution, Labrousse has made clear that he is not an advocate of any single cause or set of causes as sufficient explanations for the events of 1787–88. Four years after his epochal work on the economic crisis, he had occasion to discuss the origins of the revolutions of 1789, 1830 and 1848 in France. At one point, he exclaimed, "In each revolution, what personal, moral, and sentimental causes! What contingencies! What hazards!" Most historians are aware of this truth and it guarantees that the study of the background of the French Revolution will continue.[8]

---

[8] For Labrousse's remarks, see "1848–1830–1789: Comment naissent les révolutions," in *Actes du Congrès Historique du Centenaire de la Révolution de 1848* (Paris, 1948), p. 15.

A. Cobban, *The Myth of the French Revolution* (London, 1955); A. Cobban, "Historical Revision No. CVII: The Beginning of the French Revolution," *History*, XXX (1945), 90–98; E. Thompson, *Popular Sovereignty and the French Constituent Assembly, 1789–91* (Manchester, England, 1952); A. Goodwin, "Calonne, the Assembly of French Notables of 1787 and the Origins of the 'Révolte nobiliaire'." *English Historical Review*, LXI (1946), 329–377; J. Egret, *La Révolution des Notables: Mounier et les Monarchiens* (Paris, 1950); J. Egret, "Les origines de la Révolution en Bretagne, (1788–89)," *Revue Historique*, CCXIII (1955), 189–216; M. G. Hutt, "The Role of the Curés in the Estates General of 1789," *Journal of Ecclesiastical History*, VI (1955), 190–220; C. B. Rogers, *The Spirit of Revolution in 1789* (Princeton, 1949); P. H. Beik,

Labrousse, as most historians discussing the Revolution, stays within the boundaries of France, or considers other countries only as they affect the background or the course of events in France. There promises to be a new emphasis in the background of the French Revolution, one which places it in a pattern of a revolutionary era in Western Europe and its colonies. The colonial wars of the eighteenth century were world wars, and it is suggested that, beginning perhaps in the last third of the century, the strains on old institutions in an essentially unified Western society led to a series of radical changes not only in France and America, but throughout the Western World. The background of the French Revolution had an important center in France, but developments in France were not the whole story. As for the results of this revolutionary era in the West, we are still working them out.[9]

## For General Reading

The works cited in the footnotes are intended to give a sampling of the range of historical opinion during the past twenty years. With few exceptions, they are concerned with some special aspects

The French Revolution Seen from the Right (Philadelphia, 1956); F. Braesch, *1789, L'année cruciale* (Paris, 1941); G. Rudé, "The Outbreak of the French Revolution," *Past and Present*, no. 8 (1955), 28–42; P. H. Meyer, "The French Revolution and the Legacy of the Philosophes," *French Review*, XXX (1957), 429–434; G. H. McNeil, "The Cult of Rousseau and the French Revolution," *Journal of the History of Ideas*, VI (1945), 197–213; G. H. McNeil, "The Anti-Revolutionary Rousseau," *American Historical Review*, LVIII (1953), 808–823; P. Bastid, "Sieyès et les philosophes," *Revue de Synthèse*, XVII (1939), 137–157; B. F. Hyslop, "French Gild Opinion in 1789," *American Historical Review*, XLIV (1939); 252–271; B. C. Shafer, "Bourgeois Nationalism in the Pamphlets on the Eve of the French Revolution," *Journal of Modern History*, X (1938), 31–50; R. R. Palmer, "The National Idea in France Before the Revolution," *Journal of the History of Ideas*, I (1940), 95–101; R. R. Palmer, "The Dubious Democrat: Thomas Jefferson in Bourbon France," *Political Science Quarterly*, LXXII (1957), 388–404.

[9] R. R. Palmer, "The World Revolution of the West, 1763–1801," *Political Science Quarterly*, LXIX (1954), 1–14; "Reflections on the French Revolution," *ibid.*, LXVII (1952), 64–80; see also the extensive references in Palmer's "Recent Interpretations of the Influence of the French Revolution," *Journal of World History*, II (1954), 173–195.

J. Godechot, *La grande nation: l'expansion révolutionnaire de la France dans le monde, 1789–1799* (2 vols.; Paris, 1956); M. Kraus, *The Atlantic Civilization: Eighteenth-century Origins* (Ithaca, 1949); B. Hyslop, "French Jacobin Nationalism and Spain," in *Nationalism and Internationalism: Essays inscribed to C. J. H. Hayes* (New York, 1950); R. Herr, *The Eighteenth-century Revolution in Spain* (Princeton, 1958).

of eighteenth-century France. There are, however, some general works in English which might be of interest to those students who wish to go beyond their texts. Some of these have the further virtue of being published in inexpensive paperbacked editions (see below).

The best single brief account of the background of the Revolution is G. Lefebvre's *Quatre-Vingt-Neuf*, translated by R. R. Palmer as *The Coming of the French Revolution* (Princeton, 1947). R. W. Greenlaw (ed.), *The Economic Origins of the French Revolution: Poverty or Prosperity?* (Boston, 1958), provides essays, some not available elsewhere in English, with a wider scope than the title implies.

For studies covering a wider range of the eighteenth century than France: M. Beloff, *The Age of Absolutism, 1660–1815* (New York, 1954); L. Gershoy, *From Despotism to Revolution* (New York, 1944); J. O. Lindsay (ed.), *The Old Regime, 1713–1763*, (Vol. VII, *The New Cambridge Modern History* [Cambridge, 1957]); J. M. Wallace-Hadrill and J. McManners (eds.), *France: Government and Society* (London, 1957); M. Kraus, *The Atlantic Civilization: Eighteenth-century Origins* (Ithaca, 1949); C. Brinton, *The Anatomy of Revolution* (New York, 1952). Finally, few persons have surveyed the literature on the Revolution without failing to be impressed again with A. de Tocqueville's classic, first published in 1856, *The Old Regime and the French Revolution* (New York, 1955).

For collections of source materials, valuable for both teacher and student: I. Berlin, *The Age of Enlightenment: The Eighteenth-century Philosophers* (New York, 1955); L. L. Snyder, *The Age of Reason* (New York, 1956); C. Brinton, *The Portable Age of Reason Reader* (New York, 1956); L. Gershoy, *The Era of the French Revolution, 1789–99; Ten Years that Shook the World* (New York, 1957); J. H. Stewart, *A Documentary Survey of the French Revolution* (New York, 1951). The Gershoy and Stewart collections have introductory essays and documents on the background of the Revolution, as well as material carrying events up to Napoleon.

*Inexpensive Paperbacks Available*

I. Berlin, *The Age of Enlightenment: The Eighteenth-century Philosophers* (New American Library)

C. Brinton, *The Anatomy of Revolution* (Vintage)

A. de Tocqueville, *The Old Regime and the French Revolution* (Anchor)

L. Gershoy, *The Era of the French Revolution, 1789–99: Ten Years That Shook the World* (Anvil)

R. W. Greenlaw, *The Economic Origins of The French Revolution: Poverty or Prosperity?* (Heath)

M. Kraus, *The North Atlantic Civilization* (Anvil)

G. Lefebvre, *The Coming of the French Revolution* (Vintage)

L. L. Snyder, *The Age of Reason* (Anvil)

E. Burke, *Reflections on the Revolution in France* (Gateway)

E. Cassirer, *Philosophy of the Enlightenment* (Beacon)

D. Diderot, *Rameau's Nephew and Other Works* (Anchor)

F. Gentz, *The French and American Revolutions Compared* (Gateway)

F. E. Manuel, *The Age of Reason* (Cornell)

J. J. Rousseau, *The Social Contract* (Gateway)

J. J. Rousseau, *Confessions* (Penguin)

J. J. Rousseau, *Emile* (Barron)

Voltaire, *The Portable Voltaire: Candide, Zadig, Micromegas, selections from Philosophical Dictionary and Other Works* (Viking)

# PAMPHLETS *Published by the*

## SERVICE CENTER FOR TEACHERS OF HISTORY

*Order From:* THE MACMILLAN COMPANY, Department 47(
60 Fifth Avenue, New York 11, New York

*How to Order:* Cash must accompany all orders of $5.00 or less. I
larger orders we will gladly bill you or your organization

On quantity orders for single or assorted titles the following discour
are offered:

| | |
|---|---|
| orders for $10.00-$49.99 | 10% discount |
| orders for $50.00-$99.99 | 15% discount |
| orders for $100.00 or more | 20% discount |

Please specify title and quantity. Make checks payable to the Macmill
Company. Quantity discounts apply only if order is addressed specifica
to Department 470 of the Macmillan Company.

1. *Key to the Past: Some History Books for Pre-College Readers,* 2nd ed., by MARGARETA FAISSLER, 75c
2. *New Interpretations in American Foreign Policy,* 2nd ed., by ALEXANDER DeCONDE, 75c
3. *The South in American History,* by OTIS A. SINGLETARY, 75c
4. *Industrial Revolution: Interpretations and Perspectives,* by ERIC E. LAMPARD, 75c
5. *Civil War and Reconstruction,* 2nd ed., by HAL BRIDGES, 50c
6. *The American Revolution: A Review of Changing Interpretations,* by EDMUND S. MORGAN, 50c
7. *The Colonial Period in Latin American History,* by CHARLES GIBSON, 50c
8. *The American Frontier,* by RAY A. BILLINGTON, 50c
9. *Jacksonian Democracy,* by CHARLES G. SELLERS, JR., 50c
10. *The Progressive Movement, 1900-1920: Recent Ideas and New Literature* by GEORGE E. MOWRY, 50c
11. *Greek and Roman History,* by MORTIMER CHAMBERS, 50c
12. *The Middle West,* by HARRY R. STEVENS, 50c
13. *History of Science,* by MARIE BOAS, 50c
14. *The Nature and Practice of State and Local History,* by PHILIP D. JORDAN, 75c
15. *Chinese History: A Bibliographic Review,* by CHARLES O. HUCKER, 75c
16. *New Interpretations of American Colonial History,* 2nd ed., by LOUIS B. WRIGHT, 50c
17. *The History of India: Its Study and Interpretation,* by ROBERT I. CRANE, 75c
18. *The Interpretation of Renaissance Humanism,* by WILLIAM J. BOUWSMA, 50c
19. *Recent Trends and New Literature in Canadian History,* by ROBIN W. WINKS, 75c
20. *Nationalism: Interpreters and Interpretations,* 2nd ed., by BOYD C. SHAFER, 50c
21. *The Background of the French Revolution,* by STANLEY J. IDZERDA, 50c
22. *A Style of History for Beginners,* by PAUL L. WARD, 50c
23. *The Middle Ages in Recent Historical Thought: Selected Topics,* by BRYCE LYON, 75c
24. *The Near and Middle East: An Introduction To History and Bibliography,* by RODERIC H. DAVISON, 75c
25. *The New Deal in Historical Perspective,* by FRANK FREIDEL, 50c
26. *The Far West in American History,* by HARVEY L. CARTER, 50c
27. *Five Images of Germany: Half a Century of American Views on German History,* by HENRY CORD MEYER, 75c
28. *Great Britain in the Twentieth Century,* by HENRY R. WINKLER, 50c
29. *Nineteenth-Century Europe — Crisis and Contribution,* by EUGENE N. ANDERSON, 50c

*(Continued on cover 3)*